OECD Public Governance Reviews

# Progress in Chile's Supreme Audit Institution

## REFORMS, OUTREACH AND IMPACT

This work is published under the responsibility of the Secretary-General of the OECD. The opinions expressed and arguments employed herein do not necessarily reflect the official views of OECD member countries.

**Please cite this publication as:**
OECD (2016), *Progress in Chile's Supreme Audit Institution: Reforms, Outreach and Impact*, OECD Public Governance Reviews, OECD Publishing, Paris.
*http://dx.doi.org/10.1787/9789264250635-en*

ISBN 978-92-64-25189-2 (print)
ISBN 978-92-64-25063-5 (PDF)

Series: OECD Public Governance Reviews
ISSN 2219-0406 (print)
ISSN 2219-0414 (online)

The statistical data for Israel are supplied by and under the responsibility of the relevant Israeli authorities. The use of such data by the OECD is without prejudice to the status of the Golan Heights, East Jerusalem and Israeli settlements in the West Bank under the terms of international law.

**Photo credits:** Cover © The Comptroller General of the Republic of Chile, by Osvaldo Cristian Rudloff Pulgar

Corrigenda to OECD publications may be found on line at: *www.oecd.org/about/publishing/corrigenda.htm*.

# Table of contents

**Executive summary** ..... 5

**Introduction** ..... 7

2013: The OECD Public Governance Review of the CGR ..... 7
2015: Progress Report on the implementation of recommendations ..... 8

**1) Improving the engagement strategy** ..... 9

Initiatives and impact since the Peer Review ..... 9

**2) Supporting internal control** ..... 17

Initiatives and impact since the Peer Review ..... 18

**3) Aligning and balancing the CGR portfolio** ..... 23

Initiatives and impact since the Peer Review ..... 24

**4) Overcoming challenges and realising impact** ..... 31

Engagement strategy ..... 31
Support to internal control ..... 32
Alignment and balance of the CGR portfolio ..... 34

**Notes** ..... 36

**Bibliography** ..... 37

**Figures**

Figure 4.1. Extent of changes in the 3 key areas in 2014 ..... 31
Figure 4.2. Challenges to realising the full potential of activities in the 3 key areas ..... 33

**Tables**

Table 1.1. Summary of previous recommendations and intended benefits: Improving the engagement strategy ..... 10
Table 1.2. Assessment of initiatives to improve the CGR's engagement strategy ..... 16
Table 2.1. Summary of previous recommendations and intended benefits: Supporting internal control ..... 18
Table 2.2. Assessment of initiatives to support internal control in Chile ..... 22
Table 3.1. Summary of previous recommendations and intended benefits: Aligning and balancing the portfolio ..... 24
Table 3.2. Assessment of initiatives to align and balance the CGR portfolio ..... 29

# Executive summary

As the Supreme Audit Institution, the Office of the Comptroller General of the Republic of Chile (CGR) has a crucial role in supporting accountability and integrity in the Chilean public sector. The CGR has demonstrated its commitment to fulfilling this role in a way that is relevant to the 21st century, integrating ambitious initiatives into its 2013-2015 strategic plan. The CGR invited the OECD to undertake a Peer Review that would assist the CGR in delivering on its goals. The Review subsequently explored how the CGR's audit work could be adjusted to enhance the institution's relevance for and impact on a modernising State.

The OECD presents this Progress Report on the CGR's implementation of key recommendations of the Peer Review. It provides an overview of the initiatives in 2014 that have contributed to (i) improving the CGR's engagement strategy, (ii) the CGR's support to strengthening internal control in the Chilean public sector and (iii) aligning and balancing the CGR's portfolio with its strategic aims.

In a short time the CGR has introduced new activities and built upon previous initiatives that continue to support its current strategic plan. This Progress Report shows that both CGR officials and external stakeholders recognise the efforts of the CGR towards engaging its various audiences, reporting a higher frequency of engagement in 2014. The CGR signed in 2014 a Memorandum of Understanding with the Chamber of Deputies – an important achievement towards strengthening decision-making – as a result of an OECD recommendation. The External Control Function Integrated Improvement project and its 32 related initiatives, including developing strategies for specific groups, seems to be improving the understanding by CGR and its stakeholders in one another.

The OECD welcomes the CGR's engagement and communication activities of 2014 given that success in this area is largely a prerequisite for strengthening internal control and aligning its portfolio with its strategic aims. In the former case, engagement with other actors is critical in view of the need for professional co-operation amongst the various actors responsible for internal control and accountability in the Chilean public sector. The CGR exercises an important role in promoting internal control and accountability in Chile, and there is evidence of a change in its approach towards other actors also responsible, embedding greater trust in internal audit units. These initiatives may generate an added benefit of freeing capacity of the CGR to expand the roll-out of new value-added products that take a whole-of-government perspective and that have been recognised as valuable inputs to decision-making processes.

The CGR's 2014 initiatives and those planned for 2015 will bring the CGR closer yet to the OECD Peer Review recommendations and towards promulgating greater accountability and decision-making in Chile. In doing so, the CGR will continue to enhance its ability to reflect the needs and priorities of its surrounding context in its processes, products and next strategic plan. There is an opportunity for the CGR to set the bar higher yet, building on the momentum evident through this progress report.

# Introduction

## 2013: The OECD Public Governance Review of the CGR

In 2012, the OECD was invited to undertake a comprehensive assessment of the Office of the Comptroller General of the Republic of Chile (*Contraloria General de la República – CGR)*, known as the "Supreme Audit Institution" (SAI) of the Republic of Chile. The Chilean Constitution (Art. 98) establishes the CGR as an autonomous government body, which is neither an office of the Legislature nor of the Executive. Its mission is "to ensure legal compliance by the public administration through a collaborative relationship with public entities and citizens, promoting the public good through efficient institutional management to safeguard the integrity, transparency and correct use of public resources".

The CGR had undertaken, in the years prior to the OECD Public Governance Review, activities namely in the areas of (i) institutional strengthening, (ii) fostering transparency and integrity and (iii) enhancing citizen participation. The Review sought to support ongoing and future initiatives aimed at enabling the CGR to fulfil its function while contributing to a more strategic and agile Chilean Public Sector. Based on the expectations and role of the CGR, and the future priorities of both the CGR and the Chilean Public Sector, the Peer Review focused on five key areas:

- the CGR's ability to support strategic agility and rebuild trust in government
- the CGR's own strategic agility
- the CGR's engagement of stakeholders
- the CGR's prioritisation and quality assurance of audits
- the CGR's transparency and performance.

The OECD Peer Review found that the CGR works with a high level of operational independence. The CGR's efforts towards transparency and integrity are recognised, with it being ranked as the least corrupt institution in both 2012 and 2013 surveys of citizens' perceptions of corruption in their public sector institutions (Libertad y Desarrollo, 2014). The CGR's strategic plan had outlined ambitious targets to move away from stakeholders' perceptions of the CGR as focused solely on compliance, and is supported by a broad mandate to achieve this. Yet the OECD identified the CGR as interpreting its statutory functions in a restricted manner, undertaking those that are fulfilled by the Executive in most other OECD countries – namely, the preparation of the government's year end accounts and the *ex ante* control of legality.

The OECD outlined key recommendations in each of the five areas of the study. The recommendations centred mainly on the CGR aligning its processes with the aims set out in the strategic plan by balancing its portfolio, refocusing the communications plan and developing personnel and performance management. Recommendations were also made to enhance the institution's agility and transparency, the quality of its work and the introduction of new products to foster a more nuanced understanding of the role played by the CGR.

The review was a result of close collaboration between the OECD and CGR, relying on the practices shared by 12 peer SAIs and consultations with key stakeholders from the Chilean public and private sectors and civil society. The analysis was framed by relevant international standards including the International Standards and Guidance for Good Governance of the International Organisation of Supreme Audit Institutions (INTOSAI) and the COSO framework for internal control, for example. The preliminary Review was presented at the XXIII annual meeting of the OLACEFs, in December 2013, and the final in Santiago in April 2014.

## 2015: Progress Report on the implementation of recommendations

As part of its collaboration with the CGR, the OECD has developed a Progress Report to document the changes that the CGR continued or began in 2014 after the preliminary recommendations of the Peer Review were presented. The OECD has selected key areas based on their importance for accountability and integrity in the Public Sector, and for the CGR's achievements vis-a-vis its roadmap. This Progress Report outlines the advancements and efforts taken by the CGR, and the perceived impact of those efforts, in the following priority areas:

1. The CGR's engagement strategy;
2. The CGR's support to internal control in Chile; and
3. The alignment and balance of the CGR's portfolio.

A summary of all activities undertaken by the CGR in 2014 was provided by the CGR in the "Strategic Report: Implementation Status of Key Recommendations made by the OECD to the Office of the Comptroller General of the Republic of Chile" (CGR, 2015). Information was verified and is complemented by questionnaire results from CGR officials and external stakeholders of civil society, the legislature, the Executive and the Judiciary. The questionnaires were used to provide perspective on the extent and impact of changes that have been undertaken in 2014. The internal survey of 19 CGR staff in strategic roles was contextualized against responses from a survey of 11 external representatives.

# 1) Improving the engagement strategy

Stakeholder communication and engagement is necessary for the CGR to reflect citizens' needs in its strategies and operations. The OECD Public Governance Review of 2013 provided a comprehensive analysis of the CGR's engagement with auditees and internal control units throughout the audit cycle and with all stakeholders aside from individual audits.

The Review documented previous years' efforts to engage its stakeholders, using in-person and web-based tools to gather feedback and complaints from stakeholders as a way to address the needs of CGR clients and users. While being recognised for its commitment to transparency, the CGR was still widely perceived as solely taking an inspection and compliance-oriented approach. This perception pointed to a need for the CGR to target audiences in a way that ensures its communication and engagement strategies will lead to greater impact and understanding of its work.

The communication strategy at the time of the Review focused largely on citizens' engagement, particularly through the internet, and less on the Executive and Congress. The OECD pointed to opportunities to reach a broader audience base by taking steps to overcome a large digital divide and by engaging decision makers. Reaching this broader audience helps the CGR's strategic priorities to be more representative of and relevant to the needs of all stakeholders.

The OECD Peer Review made recommendations for the CGR to share and consult with stakeholders in order for the CGR to enhance its relevance, efficiency (by more streamlined and professional relationships with auditees and internal audit), quality (by understanding users' needs and feeding it into improvement processes) and usability of its work (for improved understanding by all). The recommendations and their intended benefits are summarised in Table 1.1.

## Initiatives and impact since the Peer Review

### ***Strengthening the communication strategy and enhancing communication***

#### *Broadening the communication strategy to define and understand audiences*

According to 94% percent of CGR officials surveyed for this Progress Review, the CGR made moderate or substantial changes to its engagement strategy in 2014 by both updating existing processes and developing anew. This was confirmed by over 80% of external stakeholders who reported that they experienced a moderate or substantial increase in their frequency of engagement with the CGR in the year 2014.

The surveys confirmed that the CGR has indeed changed the way it communicates with audiences. The CGR has been proactive in this area, reorienting its approach to be driven by user needs and viewing the citizen more in a role as collaborators and less as "users". Under the banner of the External Control Function Integrated Improvement Project the CGR has been active in broadening the communication and engagement strategies in the following ways:

**Table 1.1. Summary of previous recommendations and intended benefits: Improving the engagement strategy**

| Key recommendations | Intended benefits / goals of recommendations |
|---|---|
| Strengthen the communication strategy and enhance communication with all stakeholders by:<br>• broadening the communication strategy to define audiences and how they access information on audit activities and findings<br>• Enhancing the transparency of the CGR's responsibilities and assignments, including increasing the transparency of CGR's audit standards, processes and methods in general and as part of the protocols for individual audit engagements<br>• Enhancing the usability and clarity of CGR products and exploring measures to overcome digital barriers to stakeholders' access to information<br>• focusing specific attention to the Congress<br>Engaging auditees to develop a more constructive working relationship, by:<br>• Broadening the scope of information communicated with auditees throughout the audit process, including ensuring that the terms of the audit have been clearly established and communicated in order to support efficient execution and effective quality control of the audit.<br>• Formulating strategies to communicate with audited entities outside of individual audit engagements | • Demonstrate the value and increase the understanding of the CGR's work to its diverse audience within the Executive and Legislature – as well as citizens and the media – to increase its use in accountability and decision making processes<br>• Facilitate a better understanding and build confidence in CGR's working methods for auditees and other users<br>• Increase effectiveness of working in partnership with key stakeholders, including internal audit and control bodies, but also others<br>• Use a communication strategy to foster a broader understanding of common challenges and emerging risks affecting good public governance identified through the CGR's audit work |

- The CGR's Communications Unit began a redesign of the communications strategy to foster an improved relationship with external stakeholders. As part of this initiative, the CGR has begun mapping its various stakeholders in order to establish specialised engagement strategies and tools assigned for each grouping. This methodology and engagement plan takes into account the relative importance of each grouping.

- External control units are offering workshops, lectures and seminars, participation in pilot projects, roundtables with public entities to strengthen the work with CGR, exhibitions, trainings and hearings. Some interactions have focused on the nature of the subject of the audit or audit-related processes. Others were held to gather better impressions of the stakeholders' interests, needs and opinions on the CGR's work in order to identify areas for improvement and also weaknesses to be addressed through trainings. Of the 6,255 participants in CGR's 2014 events, 35.8% were from the municipal sector (up 10% on the previous year) and 59% from the public sector. All surveyed external stakeholders were aware that the CGR hosts opportunities for engagement, and 7 out of 11 had participated.

- The CGR has formed the Civil Society Council, building on successful interactions in previous years, to provide a forum for the CGR to listen to the concerns and proposals of Non-Governmental Organisations. The first two meetings were held in January and March 2015 to improve the internal resolution on which the council is founded, signed on March 10. It enables the Council members to call for a meeting of the Council. Feedback from the CGR officials that were surveyed for this Progress Report showed high hopes for this newly established partnership.
- As part of the collaborative initiative, "Sharing information to improve the fight against corruption in Chile", the CGR has consolidated interoperability of existing databases between the CGR, the Public Prosecutor's Office and the State defence Council, to improve the effectiveness, timeliness and transparency of investigation and prosecution of administrative corruption in the civil service.
- Under the Accountability and Civil Society project, the CGR has developed the "Tabla IFAF", a tool through which Non-Governmental Organisations format and present financial information, meant to provide reliable information to all stakeholders about the source, use and allocation of NGOs' resources. Training sessions have been used to disseminate and facilitate the use of this tool.
- The Citizens' portal, which the OECD Peer Review acknowledged to have been popular, has been consolidated and has seen an increase in activity. Complaints and suggestions have increased by 26% (from 2638 to 3581 from 2013 to 2014, respectively).
- Launched in December 2014, the GEO-CGR portal provides a forum for the articulation, storage, consultation and publication of geo-referenced information on the investment of resource in public works. It aims to promote social control and citizen-driven accountability by providing reliable and timely information useful for analysing and monitor resources invested in public works. Sixty-four public entities are involved in the current pilot, after which the monitoring system will be fully operational (late 2015).

The CGR's efforts to strengthen communication with stakeholders are being noticed, with 75% of CGR officials reporting that these efforts resulted in a moderate or substantial change in stakeholders' understanding of its CGR work – confirmed by 70% of external stakeholders.

### *Enhancing the transparency of the CGR's responsibilities and assignments*

At the time of the Peer Review, the OECD found that the CGR was not providing information to its stakeholders regarding its audit standards, processes and methods. A 2013 access to information study showed that the CGR's overall ranking in responding to access to information requests and the reliability and timeliness of information increased against 2012 but was still lower than the period of 2009-2011(GfK Adimark, 2013).

The 2002 modification to the CGR's Organic Law allowed the CGR to develop its own regulation on audit procedures. The new Audit Regulation was launched in January 2015, establishing main guidelines and methodological elements of its external control activities. As the audit regulations outline procedures and timelines for individual audits, feedback was sought from Executive representatives in their development phase. The audit regulations will be published on its institutional website that the CGR continues to update in structure and content, populating it with a wealth of information about its products, procedures and opinions that affect public management. A CGR official, who responded to the OECD survey, highlighted the importance of sharing such standards and regulations for raising confidence in the objectivity of CGR processes.

The Citizen Portal now documents progress of ongoing audits against the annual audit plan so that citizens may contribute to their development and provide input at various points of the process.[1] One stakeholder confirmed that the CGR had broadened the information shared concerning previous audits, through the provision of online content and meetings.

Efforts towards improving the engagement strategy are largely linked to increasing the breadth of information shared with stakeholders, and providing more frequent opportunity to interact in person outside of individual audit engagements. Standards are being shared with other SAIs (rules, processes and methods of audit), with internal control units, with the Council of Government's General Internal Auditors (*Consejo de Auditoría Interna General de Gobierno* - CAIGG) and with Executive branch regulations officers.

CGR officials noted that their in-person engagement of stakeholders throughout the audit process only increased moderately in relation to the previous year but that over a five-year period changes were substantial. The CGR's engagement of audited entities throughout the audit process is discussed in more detail below.

### *Enhancing the clarity of CGR work and overcoming digital barriers*

The CGR has taken steps, albeit somewhat limited, towards improving the clarity and usability of its work, with particular emphasis being placed on updating online content and the efficiency of its portals. Improvements have also been made to the systematisation of the underlying system through which the CGR compiles its audit findings, SICA 4.0 (*Sistema Integrado para el Control de Auditorias)*, promoting an improvement in the accuracy of audit findings and clarity in their presentation. The CGR is attempting to improve the clarity of executive summaries so they are better understood by stakeholders. Though the CGR uses style guides for its reports, feedback from external stakeholders highlighted that the CGR could make audit reports and communications more user-friendly, and that infographics would be an illustrative and clear way of representing otherwise complex information.

The CGR will also be introducing later in 2015 a Citizens' Mobile app for smart phones that citizens will be able to use to lodge complaints and suggestions. Recognising that Chile faces a substantial digital divide, with low levels of broadband penetration,[2] having additional channels for communication with the CGR is an important step in reaching broader audiences and overcoming digital barriers.

### *Focusing specific attention on the Congress*

On 12 December, 2014, the CGR signed a Memorandum of Understanding with the National Congress, whereby the Comptroller General will give a public account to the House in June of each year. The Comptroller General will outline main findings of relevant reports and observations, including those that have and have not been addressed, prior to the discussion of the Draft Budget for the following year. In addition, the

Comptroller General participates in Congressional meetings when periodically invited to the Chamber of Deputies to review bills, spending or when summoned to present specific audit findings.

CGR officials confirmed that there has been improved co-ordination and greater attention paid to parliamentarians, more participation and assistance provided from members of parliament to regional audit offices, and increased information sharing between Congress members to the CGR. Additionally, the CGR distributes a Municipal eNewsletter and eNewsletter on the budget execution of Central Government, which is also made available to parliamentarians.

### *Engaging auditees to develop a more constructive working relationship*

Of the five audited entities represented in the external survey, all experienced an increase in interaction between their institution and the CGR in 2014. The extent varied however, with one audited entity reporting a substantial increase in interaction, three reporting a moderate increase, and one reporting a limited increase. The mechanisms through which this interaction occurred included seminars and meetings outside of individual audit engagements, where specific audited-related topics were covered or processes piloted. The CGR has also made efforts to share more information about the audit process, as discussed below.

#### *Broadening the scope of information communicated with auditees throughout the audit process*

A constructive and professional working relationship with auditees and internal audit is important for efficiency and quality of audit assignments as well as for the system in which the CGR works. Auditee perceptions of the CGR as overly focused on compliance may have been partly due to a lack of clarity in audit proceedings. Limited interaction between auditors and auditees masks the importance of the audit for the broader governance context. Peer Review recommendations to improve working relations between the two groups were made around the following subjects.

(i) Communication materials related to the audit

At the time of the OECD Peer Review, the CGR's audit engagements began with a formal notice of the initiation of an audit, between one and three months in advance, and an initial meeting with the head of the public entity that could be held within one day's notice. The new audit regulations require the CGR to inform the auditee of the origin (planned or unplanned), the objective of the audit, the timeline and the reports to be issued as a result. Sharing this information gives legitimacy to CGR methodology, and confidence in the CGR's objectivity in selecting auditees and audit subjects.

The new audit regulations require the CGR to communicate, at the beginning of each year, the initiation of all audits by entity to be conducted in that year. This is a departure from the previous practice of notifying auditees of the commencement of individual audits by written procedure. In addition, the annual operating plan is now made available on the CGR website for full transparency of its planned activities. Given that the CGR previously thought of this information as privileged and withheld it to maintain a surprise element of its audit engagements, this change demonstrates a greater willingness on the part of the CGR to share useful information.

One stakeholder suggested that there remains a lack of clarity in the objectives in the reviewing material provided prior to an audit. This points to the need for continued efforts in improving the clarity and quality of communication materials in tandem with increasing their scope.

(ii) In person interaction around the individual audit

Of the 5 auditees that responded to the Progress Review survey, one auditee experienced an increase in interaction with the CGR pre, during and post audit. One respondent to this OECD survey saw an increase in the pre-audit phase and another during the audit. Two however, did not experience an increase in 2014 in the interaction throughout the audit cycle, suggesting that their increase in interaction (as reported above) was limited to that outside of the individual audit engagement. The auditee who reported an increase in engagement prior to the audit suggested that there could be an improvement in the communication of the auditors involved and further explanation of the review process. This is important to highlight given that the new audit regulations do not require the participation of auditors at inception meetings.

The auditee who experienced an increase in interaction during the audit suggested that the CGR consider holding meetings to communicate the findings prior to their formulisation in writing. This may be linked to other stakeholder comments that the limited time provided to the audited entities to respond to findings makes it difficult to process the information and, later, to implement recommendations.

(iii) Communication around audit findings

The OECD Peer Review found that 7 of 11 peer SAIs had specific auditee strategies, all of which required the SAI to summarise key challenges and risks facing the auditee that the SAI would want to address.[3] Ninety-two percent of CGR officials believe that communicating recurring trends and issues has a moderate to substantial impact on making audited entities more aware of the issues that their entity and other entities face.

Auditees that were surveyed reported that there was clarity in the audit findings and recommendations made by the CGR, but one asserted that a wider group may not understand the information published, making a recommendation to include infographics and displays to make it more easily understood. A further recommendation made was to update and streamline the forms and avenues through which audited entities respond to observations.

These stakeholder concerns around clarity in communication of audit findings and issues may be addressed by the methodology that CGR is developing to communicate with auditees about recurring issues in its entity in a more systematic way, discussed below. To this end the CGR is piloting consolidated reports whereby main audit findings, issues and suggested solutions are clarified.

### *Engaging auditees outside of individual audits*

INTOSAI (2010) guidance on *How to Increase the Use and Impact of Audit Reports* suggests that the relationship between SAIs and the auditee is an ongoing one that reaches beyond individual audit engagements. While the CGR did not have an auditee strategy at the time of the Peer Review, external control units are mapping stakeholders and gathering insight through meetings to develop group-specific strategies. This includes auditees.

External control units began conducting workshops with auditees to gather their opinions on CGR work. These workshops have the reciprocal benefit of assisting audited entities with overcoming identified problems, as well as fostering a greater appreciation for CGR work. Additionally, it enables the CGR to identify weaknesses in its operations to be addressed through trainings.

CGR officials recognise that the consolidation of External Control Units has led to a greater understanding and knowledge of entities, but the broader improvement of this acquisition of knowledge is ongoing. Four of five stakeholders confirmed they experienced moderate or substantial increase in how well the CGR understands their entity, with one reporting that there was no change.

**Table 1.2. Assessment of initiatives to improve the CGR's engagement strategy**

| Summary of key recommendations from the 2013-2014 OECD Peer Review | CGR officials' perceptions of changes in 2014? | Impact for CGR staff? | Impact for external stakeholders? | Main initiatives of 2014 | According to CGR officials: what are the challenges to realising full potential of these ongoing initiatives? |
|---|---|---|---|---|---|
| Strengthen the communication strategy and enhance communication with all stakeholders, by:<br>• Defining and understanding audiences<br>• Enhancing the transparency of the CGR's responsibilities and assignments<br>• Enhancing the usability and clarity of CGR products and exploring measures to overcome digital barriers<br>• Focusing specific attention on the Congress<br><br>Engaging auditees to develop a more constructive working relationship, by:<br>• Broadening the scope of information communicated with auditees<br>• Communicating with audited entities outside of individual audit engagements | What is the extent of the changes in this area in 2014?<br><br>None: 0<br>Limited: 6%<br>Moderate: 42%<br>**Substantial: 53%**<br>No comment: 0<br><br>What did these changes entail?<br><br>Both consolidation of existing and development of new processes | What impact have these changes (if any) to the CGR's engagement strategy had on the understanding and use of CGR's work by stakeholders?<br><br>None: 0<br>Limited: 26%<br>**Moderate: 42%**<br>Substantial: 32%<br>No comment: 0 | In 2014, to what extent did your understanding and use of CGR's audit work increase?<br><br>None: 20%<br>Limited: 10%<br>**Moderate: 50%**<br>Substantial: 20%<br>No comment: 0 | External Control Function Integrated Improvement Project<br><br>Redesign of communications strategy and mapping of stakeholders<br><br>Establishment of the Civil Society Council<br><br>Launch of the new audit regulations<br><br>Development of a Citizens' App for mobile phones<br><br>MOU signed with Congress<br><br>Ongoing trainings and workshops | Other<br>Lack of funding<br>Lack of awareness<br>Lack of buy-in from externals<br>Lack of buy-in from internals<br>Lack of time<br>Lack of capacities/know-how<br>Lack of leadership<br>None<br>0 2 4 6 8 10 |

# 2) Supporting internal control

The CGR's responsibilities for internal audit are shared with the Council of Government's General Internal Auditors (CAIGG). The CGR is responsible for supervising and guiding the activities of internal audit units within public entities, while the CAIGG is formally responsible for proposing policies, plans, programmes and internal control measures for the public administration. The two co-ordination bodies began working together in 2012 to avoid confusion or overlap of requirements of auditees.

The OECD Peer Review found that CGR's activities, and its portfolio more broadly, was responding in many ways to weaknesses in the overall control system in Chile, given *i)* the absence of independent administrative courts; *ii)* the absence of a legal mandate and professionalisation of the function of internal audit/internal control; and *iii)* concerns over the independence and professionalisation of internal audit units and legal units. The Chilean Government is currently redefining the structure and functioning of the internal audit model.

In this context, the OECD Peer Review provided a comprehensive analysis of the CGR's *ex ante* control of legality - the *toma de razón* - given that it remains an important control for the preservation of law and order in Chile. The *toma de razón* (TdR) is a preventive, *ex ante* verification of the legality of certain administrative acts, exclusively focused on legal compliance with the spectrum of national and applicable international legal frameworks. It is mainly linked to administrative acts concerning personnel, public works and acquisitions.

The *ex ante* control function is executed by the CGR, unlike in other peer countries where it is the responsibility of the Executive and not the SAI[4]. *Ex ante* control has the advantage of being able to prevent damage to the State before it occurs (INTOSAI, 1977, Section 2). The broad application of the TdR, however, risks undermining incentives for leadership of public entities to strengthen internal control, if they rely on the CGR's *ex ante* control instead of employing control mechanisms to verify acts' compliance with appropriate legal frameworks. Alternatively, public entities may pay excessive attention to the acts subject to *ex ante* control, duplicating efforts and incurring opportunity costs for both parties. The OECD Peer Review made suggestions for approaching and applying the *toma de razón* in a way that could strengthen the internal control in Chile, noting that changes to the *toma de razón* should be made in tandem with broader public administration efforts. Table 2.1 summarises the main recommendations and their intended benefits.

**Table 2.1. Summary of previous recommendations and intended benefits: Supporting internal control**

| Specific recommendations | Intended benefits / goals |
|---|---|
| Proactively support efforts to consolidate an independent, capable and efficient system of internal control in the Chilean public sector, by:<br>• Conducting assessments of strengths and weaknesses, challenges and opportunities of existing mechanisms, including internal control and legal units, and promote policy discussion to facilitate decision making<br>• Providing public entities with structured information on recurring issues by type of administrative act or public entity in order to support the identification of ways to improve administrative decision making<br>• Providing guidance and support for the professionalisation and capacity building of internal control, taking into account the Institute of Internal Auditor's International Standards for the Professional Practice of Internal Auditing<br>• Utilising *ex ante* audit assignments to enhance the maturity of risk based internal control within public entities and to develop good management practices, including by: integrating the automation of the CGR's *ex ante* audit assignments with government management ICT systems and utilising exemptions to the CGR's *ex ante* audit assignments in order to incentivise sustained improvement in decision making and internal control | Assist in the development of a stronger institutional control framework that can provide better guidance and capacity for improving strategic agility in the public sector.<br><br>Incentivise public managers to strengthen internal control and the maturity of their management systems as well as to focus greater attention on the appropriate competencies of officials occupying roles in legal, financial, procurement and human resource management units.<br><br>Convergence of Chile towards international standards in internal audit and control |

## Initiatives and impact since the Peer Review

### *Proactively supporting efforts to consolidate internal control*

CGR officials felt that the extent of changes in the CGR's approach to reinforcing internal control in 2014 was only limited (33%)[5]. Changes were incremental, being attributed mostly to the consolidation of existing activities and processes as opposed to introduction of new.

In fulfilment of their co-ordination role, the CGR has put emphasis on its communications portal shared between the CGR and internal control units of the administration. It serves as a means to promote good practices, share lessons learned and address the questions of internal audit units. Further, it aims to foster a better understanding on the complementarity of the roles of internal and external audit and the importance in, and capacity for, fulfilling their respective control responsibilities. Since the review the CGR has:

- Continued to post on its portal CGR news, legal opinions, court of accounts' decisions regarding the actions of internal auditors, frequently used norms, accounting standards, INTOSAI standards, documents of interest and a directory of approximately 1 000 government internal auditors.
- Placed attention on remaining responsive to questions from internal audit or control units that are channelled through the portal. The average response time for inquiries from public sector entities is five working days. In 2014, the majority of questions had to do with correct interpretation of laws related to human resource

management (e.g. substitutions, subrogations and potential conflicts of interests), finance (expenditure allocations corresponding to fines and costs of representation) and institutional functions and procedures.

The CGR did, however, introduce a new initiative that provides other actors, namely citizens, with a tool to provide oversight and control. The CGR launched, in December 2014, the GEO-CGR portal that stores and allows for the publication, articulation and consultation of geo-referenced information on the investment of resources in public works, with the aim of promoting social control by providing citizens and other users with the tools to monitor reliable and timely and information categorised by territory. Users can lodge complaints and make suggestions on control, facilitating the easier and more active participation of citizens in ensuring control in the public sector.

*Conducting assessments of internal control mechanisms and promoting discussion to facilitate decision making*

As the CGR develops new methodologies for evaluating internal control more broadly, it has begun piloting questionnaires to assess the internal control environment to confirm or adjust the CGR's confidence interval in the control environment from its 95% level of confidence. The results of this testing can be found on the SICA 4.0 platform.

This preliminary testing would provide valuable information for the systematic evaluation of internal control mechanisms, which the CGR has yet to explore in depth.

*Providing public entities with information on recurring issues to support evidence-based decision making*

The survey of CGR officials showed that 92% of surveyed officials believe that communicating recurring issues has a substantial or moderate impact on ensuring that audited entities are more aware of them. CGR's stakeholders agreed that it is useful to receive guidance based on an accumulation of insights from cross-cutting audits. This heightens the level of insight provided from individual audit observations drawing out trends and risks that are being detected within their entity and across entities. Of the 5 audited entities engaged in this progress report, 3 confirmed that the CGR already shared information on recurring issues in their entity and provided suggested solutions to remedy them. All 3 that reported these suggested solutions were highly useful in addressing recurring issues.

The impact of the CGR's work in supporting internal control depends, however, on the entity's ability and willingness to implement recommendations aligned with issues detected in audits. External stakeholders reported that the greatest drawback of the CGR's existing follow-up processes was an insufficient amount of time allotted for the entity to respond to, let alone to remedy, recommendations. CGR's focus on compliance of deadlines, according to one stakeholder, does not contribute to the application of solutions that are sustainable or effective. One stakeholder recommended that the CGR standardise its criteria for related judicial proceedings, in light of the fact that entities have broader general public administration criteria that is different and may give rise to confusion on the part of the entity.

In the second half of 2015, internal control units of the Executive will partly acquire responsibility of verifying compliance with the follow-up requirements established in CGR's 2012 follow-up model, by examining the correction of minor observations and informing the CGR's follow-up units on their results. This has the double benefit of expanding the CGR's follow-up coverage as well as empowering internal control units.

Internal control units will receive, starting in 2015, consolidated follow-up reports that list all observations to be corrected and their respective cut-off dates. The improved SICA 4.0 information system enables the CGR to process and synthesise various audit findings in order to generate rankings of public sector entities and municipalities. This synthesis takes into account recommendations that have been rectified and disciplinary proceedings associated with entities. This reflects a move from the act of monitoring audit reports to monitoring observations more broadly, which will remain active until corrected, regardless of their date or association to any one individual audit.

### *Providing guidance and support for the professionalisation and capacity of internal control*

Co-ordination and co-operation between SAIs and public sector internal auditors can support effective and efficient audit and non-audit assignments by both parties, but should be managed to avoid undermining confidentiality, independence and objectivity (INTOSAI, 2010b).

Prior to the OECD review, the CGR limited its in-person interaction with internal audit units to its annual meeting held to support ongoing communications and institutional relations between the two. In 2011, the CGR created an online Portal for Internal Audit Units in order to support communications and share information with internal auditors in the central and municipal government.

Since the Review, the CGR has increased its interactions with internal audit and control units, and occasionally with the CAIGG, in meetings, seminars and training sessions such as the seminar "A different contribution to governance: internal control". The themes and aims of these meetings have included strengthening mutual co-operation and empowering all groups to ensure better monitoring of observations and findings. CGR officials reported that there has been a great interest on the part of audited entities to participate. In January 2015, the CGR brought international experts together with internal control units for a well-attended forum on strengthening internal control.

In its role in co-ordinating internal audit in Chile, the CGR is leading the public sector's convergence towards International Public Sector Accounting Standards (IPSAS) (*Normas Internacionales de Contabilidad del Sector Público*, NICSP, in Spanish), making it available on the internal audit portal and providing training. Engagement has been an important part of each phase of IPSAS integration. The CGR's Division of Financial Analysis has requested the involvement of internal control units to assist in the development of a plan for the regularization of fixed assets, as a pilot phase of this convergence.

### *Utilising ex ante audit assignments to enhance risk-based internal control*

To mitigate potential obstacles posed to strengthening internal control by the broad application of the TdR, the OECD Review recommended that the CGR consider using exemptions of TdR more regularly to "graduate" acts or entities, and further integrating the automation of the CGR's *ex ante* audit assignments into government ICT systems.

The CGR undertook a study, spanning 2012 to 2014, to estimate the economic value of the TdR, along with other CGR work products, honing in on acts of administration for infrastructure, personnel and legal functions. The preliminary findings highlight the potential impacts of the 2008 changes to the TdR function, including that exemptions to the TdR by financial threshold may incentivise fragmentation of contracts to avoid being subject to *ex ante* control. The study also indicated success in developing "framework agreements", which enable public sector entities to acquire services from a pre-approved list for up to three years without requiring additional *ex ante* approval. The agreements have reduced the number of acts subject to TdR and, according to that specific calculation, yielded a high economic return. This cost-benefit analysis could be undertaken for acts in other administrative areas subject to TdR, with an adjustment in the cost-side calculation, in order to draw broader policy implications on the value of the TdR *vis-a-vis* other CGR products (CGR, 2014a).

As a core element of its work, the CGR had taken a number of actions to enhance the timeliness and consistency in the way it conducted the *ex ante* control of legality (TdR), particularly following 2008 modifications. The legislative respondent involved in the Progress Review suggested that the TdR remains important for avoiding errors that could be incurred by public sector officials, but points out that it is a slow process. With effectiveness and efficiency in mind, the CGR launched in 2009 its Public Administration Personnel Information and Control System (*Sistema de Información y Control del Personal de la Administración del Estado* - SIAPER). What began as a database for the CGR on personnel administration and human resource decisions has transformed into a platform for the digitalisation of the TdR. The SIAPER TRA (SIAPER *Toma de Razón Automática*) module became operational in its pilot phase in 2014, enabling 20 public sector entities to process TdR online for matters related to personnel.

The automation of SIAPER for personnel matters marks an important change in the CGR's approach towards *ex ante* control, shifting the responsibility of validating and monitoring all acts from the CGR to public entities that are now responsible for taking appropriate action. This embeds trust in entities to implement internal controls appropriately, increasing the maturity of the internal control system, and is complemented by the *ex post* function which remains to detect instances where entities have failed to do so appropriately. This major change, which required the legislation (law 20 766)[6] to be modified in regards to the way the CGR relates to administration, has enabled the CGR to reallocate resources in order to undertake other work that is important for increasing the maturity of other key areas of public sector governance.

## Table 2.2. Assessment of initiatives to support internal control in Chile

| Summary of key recommendations from the 2013-2014 OECD Peer Review | CGR officials' perceptions of changes in 2014? | Impact for CGR staff? | Impact for external stakeholders? | Main initiatives of 2014 | According to CGR officials: what are the challenges to realising full potential of these ongoing initiatives? |
|---|---|---|---|---|---|
| Proactively support efforts to consolidate an independent, capable and efficient system of internal control in the Chilean public sector, by:<br>• Conducting assessments of existing control mechanisms, including internal control and legal units, and promote policy discussion to facilitate decision making<br>• Providing public entities with structured information on recurring issues to support the improvement of administrative decision making<br>• Supporting for the professionalisation and capacity building of internal control<br>• Utilising *ex ante* audit assignments to enhance the maturity of risk based internal control within public entities | What is the extent of the changes in this area in 2014?<br><br>None: 0<br>**Limited: 33%**<br>Moderate: 22%<br>Substantial: 22%<br>No comment: 17%<br><br>What did these changes entail?<br><br>Mostly consolidation of existing activities and processes | What impact have any changes to the CGR's approach to internal control had on reinforcing internal control in Chile?<br><br>None: 5%<br>Limited: 26%<br>**Moderate: 42%**<br>Substantial: 11%<br>No comment: 16% | What impact does the CGR have on strengthening internal control in the public sector?<br><br>None: 9%<br>Limited: 9%<br>Moderate: 9%<br>**Substantial: 73%**<br>No comment: 0 | Updated portal shared with internal audit units<br><br>Provided consolidated reports and communicating around recurring issues<br><br>Leading the implementation of IPSAS standards on accounting<br><br>Piloting the SIAPER TRA system for TdR acts related to personnel (20 public sector entities)<br><br>Launched the GEO-CGR portal<br><br>Continued development of consolidated follow-up reports (2014) and follow-up processes (for 2015) | Other<br>Lack of funding<br>Lack of awareness<br>Lack of buy-in from externals<br>Lack of buy-in from internals<br>Lack of time<br>Lack of capacities/know-how<br>Lack of leadership<br>None<br>0 2 4 6 8 |

# 3) Aligning and balancing the CGR portfolio

International Standards of Supreme Audit Institutions (ISSAI) define three general types of public sector auditing: financial, compliance and performance. As discussed above, a core element of the CGR's portfolio is the *ex ante* control of legality focused on the legality and compliance of proposed acts. The CGR's *ex post* audit assignments focus primarily on the compliance with legal standards in order to safeguard public funds and promote administrative integrity. The CGR had looked at the identification of errors and efficiencies, but not the root causes of shortcomings.

Prior to the OECD Review, the CGR had been changing its *ex post* compliance audit assignments to provide a more holistic approach of public entities and government programmes. For example, in 2008 the CGR introduced national and transversal audit programmes. National audits focus on the same subject within a single central public entity that has activities throughout the entire country. Transversal audits focus on the same subject across a range of centralised and decentralised entities that share a common hierarchical or financial dependence with the same central public entity.

The CGR does not audit the end of year financial statement of individual public entities or the government more broadly.[7] The case of Chile is different than that of many SAIs insofar as it is the CGR, rather than the Executive, which consolidates the year-end government report using the information provided by public entities and municipalities. The OECD recommended introducing an audit of the annual financial statements issued by individual public entities that would be linked to the timetable for budget preparation.

The CGR does not formally conduct performance audits, making it an outlier in relation to the benchmark SAIs in the Peer Review, though issues of economy, efficiency and effectiveness may be appear in individual audit engagements in an *ad hoc* manner. The CGR does not audit the reliability of financial reporting, or the reliability of non-financial information. While internal audit units within individual public entities may provide reasonable assurance of the reliability and timeliness of non-financial performance information, this is not guaranteed.

A key challenge that the CGR faced was in communicating the findings of its various audit assignments in a way that elevated them to the attention of government authorities, public officials and the general public. CGR stakeholders within the Executive and legislature, as well as representatives of civil society and the media, found it difficult to articulate what the main issues are that the CGR has raised regarding specific public entities, government sectors or management functions. Thus the recommendations in the Peer Review centred on aligning the CGR's portfolio to the strategic plan, ensuring that its work could evolve with the needs of the public sector and of Chile more broadly, as detailed in Table 3.1.

**Table 3.1. Summary of previous recommendations and intended benefits: Aligning and balancing the portfolio**

| Specific recommendations | Intended benefits / goals |
|---|---|
| Foster strategic sensitivity of emerging trends and risks affecting public governance and changing societal expectations as input into the CGR's strategic planning and institutional modernisation, including<br>• establishing capabilities and processes to continuously collect external information on current trends and risks affecting governance<br>• Matching this information with CGR sources to enable discussions internally and to prioritise *ex post* audit engagements through materiality and risk assessments<br><br>Utilise *ex post* audit assignments to enhance responsibility over the use of public resources and to assess the reliability of information generated and reported by public entities to enhance the use of this information for accountability and decision-making processes, including:<br>• Auditing the reliability of non-financial performance information together with the audit of annual financial statements<br>• Auditing whole-of-government issues that are key for the government to become more strategically agile (including decision-making systems, regulatory management practices and internal control)<br>• Delivering value-added products, presenting findings from *ex post* audit work in new ways to further engage those charged with governance, including developing products that combine the findings of different *ex post* audit assignments, demonstrating common trends and root causes across the government | Focus its audit assignments on the well-functioning of government systems and understanding the recurring problems and the root causes, rather than limiting itself to the identification of illegal acts, to better support the efforts to strengthen public governance at national and sub-national levels.<br><br>Provide valuable counsel and foresight of these trends and risks affecting public governance to those charged with governance.<br><br>Focus the attention of the legislature and citizens on the content and reliability of information that government actually produces.<br><br>Ensure that it has adequate human capital to respond to changes within the public administration (or, similarly, enable the institution to respond to emerging governance issues and to adapt to changing circumstances, rebalancing and adjusting its functions and workforce internally) |

## Initiatives and impact since the Peer Review

### *Using sensitivity to public sector trends and risks as input into strategic planning*

#### *Establishing capabilities to collect information on trends and risks affecting governance*

As part of the External Control Function Integrated Improvement Project, which includes 32 initiatives, the CGR has hosted various seminars, lectures and focus groups for the CGR to collect information on audiences and their uses of CGR work. As mentioned earlier, these efforts are recognised by external stakeholders, confirming that their engagement with the CGR has increased in 2014. All stakeholders were aware of such opportunities for interaction, and the majority (8 out of 11) had been involved in discussions on whole-of-government issues.

Building on the strides CGR had taken in restructuring its workforce, the OECD Review's recommendations centred on the need to continue restructuring in order to develop competencies that will provide the capacity for the achievement of the strategic plan in the longer-term. As the *ex ante* and *ex post* functions required somewhat different skill sets, the OECD recommended that the CGR develop and link clearly a competency management system to guide the recruitment of the capacities and capabilities needed to support the strategic plan in the long-term. The CGR has since made updates to its competency-based management model, synthesising requirements for basic and advanced skill sets associated with different positions and implementing the associated curricula through courses on various platforms (e-learning, classroom and blended and guided learning). In this context a new performance-based evaluation model is being deigned and piloted for heads of unit.

The OECD had also recommended that the CGR address the fragmentation of its human resources management, which was located across different units, with insufficient co-ordination amongst. The OECD welcomes the 2014 introduction of the People Development Area, encompassing the Personnel, Training, Welfare and Quality of Working Life Departments in order to give human resource management a more strategic and coherent focus.

The CGR is also working to improve its internal efficiency and effectiveness, establishing goals for interdivisional work in the form of "internal service agreements". These agreements require that two CGR divisions make commitments to certain products to be delivered collaboratively for which the agreed milestones and products are used as performance management criteria. It is envisioned that the CGR will develop the same type of collaborative agreement with external stakeholders, which will also link to performance objectives for CGR officials. This will enable the CGR to more easily draw horizontal conclusions and remain informed about relevant work in-house.

Finally, consolidation of a database in 2014 and 2015 will allow the CGR to efficiently draw on a more comprehensive and comparative resource base. Two new matrices on observations and on follow-up activities of entities have been developed, which better organises the relevant information derived through audits and enables ranking of the level of complexity of audit observations. It is from these matrices that the CGR has generated reports of audit findings by entity and by sector, discussed below.

### *Matching information on trends and risks with CGR audit planning, implementation and follow-up*

The CGR's prioritisation process is comprehensive, integrating materiality and risk assessments that look at government priorities (strategic perspective), the importance of an entity for national social development (social perspective), as well as characteristics of service delivery (functional perspective). Now, the CGR is integrating a deeper knowledge of audited entities and citizens for its top-down and bottom-up prioritisation process, through targeted focus groups and surveys, working to heighten the relevance and understanding of audit engagements and outcomes for all of its users.

There has also been greater space allotted towards channelling regional needs into the prioritisation of issues. The CGR allocates 55% of its capacity to planned audits, and 45% to unexpected or unplanned requests. Almost 80% of the capacity directed towards unplanned requests is directed in response to regional needs.

## *Using ex post audit to enhance responsibility over public resources*

### *Auditing the reliability of financial and non-financial performance information*

It is the CGR, rather than the Executive, which consolidates the year-end government report using the information provided by public entities and municipalities. At the time of the Peer Review it was recommended that the CGR consider reorienting its *ex post* audit assignments towards auditing the reliability of performance and non-financial information reported by entities. Streamlining financial reporting of entities and issuing observations on its reliability in a systematic and timely way strengthens the evidence base on which important budgetary decisions are made.

In its role in setting public sector accounting standards in Chile, the CGR embarked on a five year process of public sector convergence towards the International Public Sector Accounting Standards (IPSAS). Introduced in 2011 and entering into force in 2016, the IPSAS will require that 226 public entities of the Central Government (and, later, 345 municipalities) will submit financial statements in accordance with these international accounting norms. In its 2014 phase of integration, the CGR piloted IPSAS through a project on the regularization of fixed assets, requiring collaboration of various internal CGR divisions as well as senior task teams appointed in entities involved (CGR, 2014b).

The CGR's Accounting Analysis Division introduced, in 2014, three annual reports aggregating financial information on "Fiscal Funding for Higher Education" and on budget execution for the municipal and public sectors. In addition to broadening the provision of materials on financial activity of the public sector, the CGR also exposes its readers to a more systematic presentation of financial information.

These initiatives aim to lay the groundwork for entities to provide financial information in a specified format and timeframe that would allow for future and systematic analyses of the reliability of their financial reporting. The process of convergence towards IPSAS has required greater collaboration between the CGR and public administration.

The CGR does not audit the reliability of non-financial performance information. Internal audit units within individual public entities may provide reasonable assurance of the reliability and timeliness of non-financial performance information. However, this is by no means guaranteed, and can be limited by capacity and competencies that are not optimally aligned with the goals of the organisation. In response, the CGR is developing a methodology for performance audits, which includes scope for auditing the reliability of non-financial performance information as inputs.

### *Auditing key whole-of-government issues*

The OECD Peer Review recommended a two-pronged approach towards realigning its portfolio in support of its strategic plan and a strategically agile state, by developing new capacities as well as reallocating those already existing.

The Peer Review looked at the CGR's *ex post* assignments, which focused on compliance with limited to no integration of aspects of effectiveness, efficiency or economy of programmes or processes. Since 2011 the CGR has been developing a performance audit methodology, integrating ISSAI 100 and 300 and peer inputs from the region and focusing on effectiveness, efficiency and economy. The CGR has scheduled pilots for the first quarter of 2015, and has meanwhile undertaken complementary activities that aim to support a smooth implementation, including:

- Workshops aimed at exchanging practices in risk-based management of SAIs and trends in performance audit, in conjunction with OLACEFs and with financial support from the Inter-American Development Bank.

- Competency building activities for CGR officials including: Public Policy Evaluation certification for 22 officials, participation of 17 officials in OLACEFs performance audit virtual course, virtual and in-person internships with the SAI of Mexico and Performance audit certification for 4 officials run through INTOSAI's International Development Initiative.
- The 10 Systems Audits conducted in 2014 focused on assessment of services with a high impact on citizens and on public sector management, including ChileCompra, the National Emergency Office, and the National Training and Employment Service, to name a few.

CGR officials backed performance audit as an effective and necessary tool to support public sector decision makers, while others pointed out that political and financial support from the public administration will be needed for its rollout. It is interesting to note that two of the audited entities surveyed suggested that the usefulness of assessments of their efficiency, effectiveness and economy in supporting their entities' operations would be limited. However, from the legislative representative perspective, these assessments would be considered very useful for decision-making and accountability in the public sector. In particular, it would allow for the faster creation and convergence towards higher standards in the public sector.

Automating the SIAPER TRA is a step towards increasing the maturity of internal control mechanisms of public entities, reducing processing time and shifting the responsibility of the CGR in monitoring and verifying acts related to personnel to entities. While SIAPER only became fully operational as a pilot in 2014, CGR officials have pointed already to the impact it has had in reducing processing time and enabling the CGR to reallocate resources for more productive tasks and other priority areas. This is a welcomed advancement by external stakeholders who also pointed to the slow processing times as being a weakness in the TdR process.

### *Delivering value-added products and presenting findings in new ways*

External perceptions of the CGR's compliance orientation reflected, in part, a lack of awareness of the CGR's broader contribution to good governance. The OECD Review found that audit findings were not raised effectively to the attention of decision makers. Since then, the CGR has developed and delivered various value-added products, using insight and *ex post* audits to package work in newer and cross-cutting ways. Examples of these initiatives are detailed below.

- The CGR created in 2014 a number of reports that aggregated audit results by sector and by entity, a process which is foreseen to expand in 2015 once the information of previous years is consolidated in the aforementioned database. Of auditees that were surveyed, all 5 knew of CGR's consolidated reports. While 3 had not yet used them, 2 had accessed them and found them to be very useful for their work.
- The new observations matrix categorises findings based on their level of complexity (from highly complex to madly complex). These rankings should contextualise the observation in order to heighten the understanding of the public and to focus the attention of public entities on more complex observations.

- As detailed above, follow-up reports that compile audit observations yet to be addressed along with their respective cut-off dates will be periodically submitted to internal audit units, beginning in 2015. Internal audit units will assume greater responsibility for overseeing their implementation, highlighting greater distribution of responsibility over internal control mechanisms.

External stakeholders were asked whether they felt an online report on the status of actions taken by audited entities to remedy observations would provide incentive for audited entities to take appropriate actions. The majority of responses, including from auditees, was positive. Reservations on the matter had to do with the need to ensure that this report, as with any, is presented in a way that would facilitate reading and understanding, using plain language and infographics, where possible. As mentioned in the first section, efforts to improve the usability and accessibility of reports will not go unnoticed. External stakeholders were also asked whether these reports would make a useful tool for citizens' oversight of public administration. The impressions were that stakeholders see these reports as having greater impact on citizen oversight than they would on ensuring compliance of auditees or action against observations.

**Table 3.2. Assessment of initiatives to align and balance the CGR portfolio**

| Summary of key recommendations from the 2013-2014 OECD Peer Review | CGR officials' perceptions of changes in 2014? | Impact for CGR staff? | Impact for external stakeholders? | Main initiatives of 2014 | According to CGR officials: what are the challenges to realising full potential of these ongoing initiatives? |
|---|---|---|---|---|---|
| Foster strategic sensitivity of emerging trends and risks affecting public governance and changing societal expectations, including:<br>• Collecting external information on current trends and risks affecting governance<br>• Matching information with CGR sources to enable discussions internally and to prioritise *ex post* audit engagements<br><br>Utilise *ex post* audit assignments to enhance responsibility over the use of public resources and to assess the reliability of information, including:<br>• Auditing the reliability of non-financial performance information together with the audit of annual financial statements<br>• Auditing whole-of-government (including decision-making systems, regulatory management practices and internal control)<br>• Delivering value-added products, presenting findings from *ex post* audit work in new ways | What is the extent of the changes in this area in 2014?<br><br>None: 0<br>Limited: 5%<br>**Moderate: 53%**<br>Substantial: 31%<br>No comment: 10%<br><br>What did these changes entail?<br><br>Both consolidation of existing and development of new processes | What is the extent of the changes to the alignment and balance of the CGR's portfolio in 2014?<br><br>None: 0<br>Limited: 5%<br>**Moderate: 53%**<br>Substantial: 32%<br>No comment: 11% | In 2014, **73%** of external stakeholders interacted with the CGR to discuss issues and trends that cut across the public administration. | Provided trainings and workshops to gather information fed into prioritisation and audit planning<br><br>Continued development of a competency management system, linked to a new performance-evaluation methodology<br><br>Continued development of performance audit methodology (pilot in 2015)<br><br>Piloted new consolidated summary reports on observations and action by entity<br><br>Issued consolidated reports by sector<br><br>Developed observations and follow-up matrices | 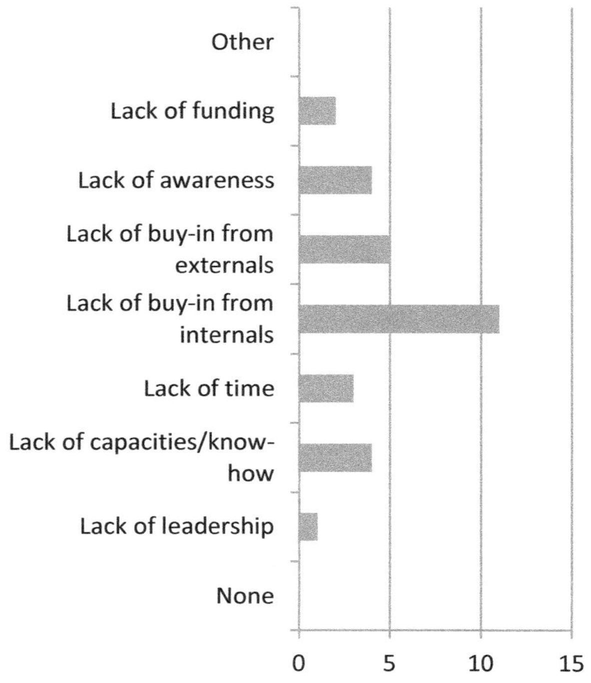  |

# 4) Overcoming challenges and realising impact

With the same commitment that inspired the CGR to subject its institution to an objective and critical Peer Review, the CGR has progressed against many of the key recommendations that were presented as a result. In a short amount of time, the CGR has built on existing processes and ongoing efforts, as well introduced completely new activities in each area that this Progress Report has focused on. Figure 1 draws attention to the extent of change within the CGR in the focus areas, based on the opinions of CGR officials. All but one official reported some form of change in 2014. This section provides insight into opportunities for the CGR to maximise the impact of their activities moving forward.

**Figure 4.1. Extent of changes in the 3 key areas in 2014**

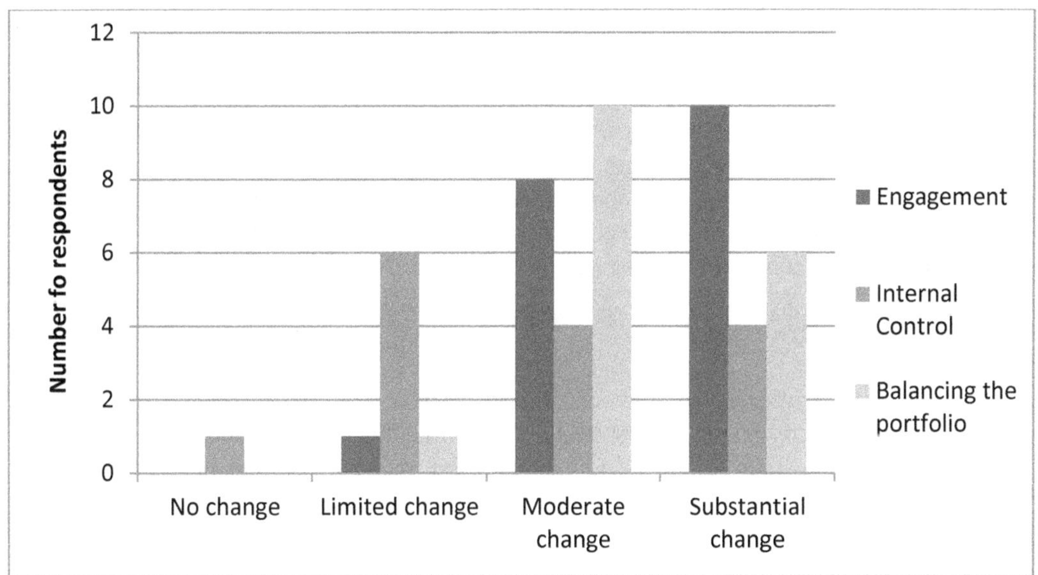


## Engagement strategy

In 2014, the CGR continued with its trend of embodying greater transparency, improving existing reforms and processes and introducing new initiatives in line with OECD recommendations. Ninety-four percent of CGR officials responding to the survey felt that a moderate or substantial change has been made in its engagement strategy in 2014, which largely has required introduction of new initiatives as well as updating old processes. Yet challenges remain.

At the outset, the CGR has changed its communication strategy to better target and understand its various audiences, sharing yet more information on its websites and public sector platforms. These efforts have been noticed. The CGR will extend its engagement with CGR stakeholders further in 2015 by sharing ongoing audits on their website, allowing citizens not only to learn about the CGR and its processes, but also to engage with individual audits in real-time.

The CGR has also expanded the breadth of information it shares with audited entities, including that of its methods and processes, which should work to break down barriers and professionalise more efficient working relationships. More frequent interactions between the CGR and audited entities is largely attributable to engagement outside of the audit process through seminars and workshops.

The CGR has taken strident steps towards improving its engagement with citizens since the OECD Peer Review, recognised by external stakeholders who applauded the CGR for their efforts in supporting greater transparency in Chile. Seventy percent of surveyed external stakeholders reported an increased understanding of the CGR in 2014, suggesting that these efforts are beginning to take effect, but that the benefits of these initiatives have not yet been filtered to all.

Due attention needs to be given to ensuring that the information gathered and shared is clear such that it translates into a true understanding of the material, and such that efforts are not futile. Stakeholders recommended further clarification, in written reports and in person, to make technical aspects more accessible to a wider audience. Ensuring that CGR material is shared and is user-friendly also requires reaching citizens beyond digital barriers. The CGR mobile app, slated to be implemented later in 2015, should assist by reaching those on smart phones that may not have internet access.

The usefulness of audit work as inputs into decision-making will depend, to a certain extent, on the openness and willingness of decision-makers to use it for this purpose. To this end, the CGR can use the momentum generated by signing an MOU with Congress to engage a wider set of decision-makers. This has been a critical step towards increasing confidence and buy-in of key actors responsible for decision and policy making in Chile.

## Support to internal control

As one of two internal audit co-ordination bodies, it is not surprising that 73% of stakeholders reported that the CGR has a substantial impact on strengthening internal control in the public sector. The CGR has made efforts to strengthen internal control to the extent that their capacity and interaction with other players will allow.

The CGR has redesigned its approach towards engaging internal audit and control units in the name of greater internal control. A significant step towards this end was in the automation of TdR for administrative personnel matters in the SIAPER system. It reflects a change in the culture around TdR and internal control, moving from a tone of distrust and of the need to have CGR monitor and verify all actions, to a culture of trust, placing the responsibility in the hands of internal control units. This is further reflected in the new follow-up processes, which will shift responsibility from the CGR to internal control units to monitor more closely an entity's actions against audit observations. This demonstrates efforts to change the way that the CGR role relates to administration and, particularly, to internal audit and control units.

External stakeholders were complimentary about the CGR's efforts in engagement and its ongoing role in strengthening internal control in Chile. Its tools and feedback mechanisms (through portals and meetings) are recognised as furthering the co-operation between internal and external control. These are aligned with the responses from CGR officials, who see the need and importance in furthering interactions through trainings and capacity building. CGR officials and external stakeholders did suggest that there has been a change in the acceptance on the part of third parties, including citizens, in their role in accountability and control, and recommended that the CGR should continue with their efforts in empowering other actors.

In view of the many actors responsible for internal control in Chile, a more holistic approach to strengthening internal control mechanisms requires activity on the part of all responsible. This may explain why CGR officials that responded to the OECD survey differed in their opinion on the extent to which changes have been made to support internal control. Thirty-three percent pointed to a limited change in their reinforcement of the internal control system, with 22% seeing a moderate changes and another 22% seeing a substantial change.

The main obstacles to realising the impacts of ongoing and future initiatives were reported to be difficulties in getting buy-in from external stakeholders and a lack of awareness on the topic more broadly. Getting buy-in from internal stakeholders was not considered to be a substantial obstacle, as it appeared to be in for other themes in this Progress Review (Figure 4.2). However, officials point to a lack of time as a challenge in realising the full impact of their work in this field.

**Figure 4.2. Challenges to realising the full potential of activities in the 3 key areas**

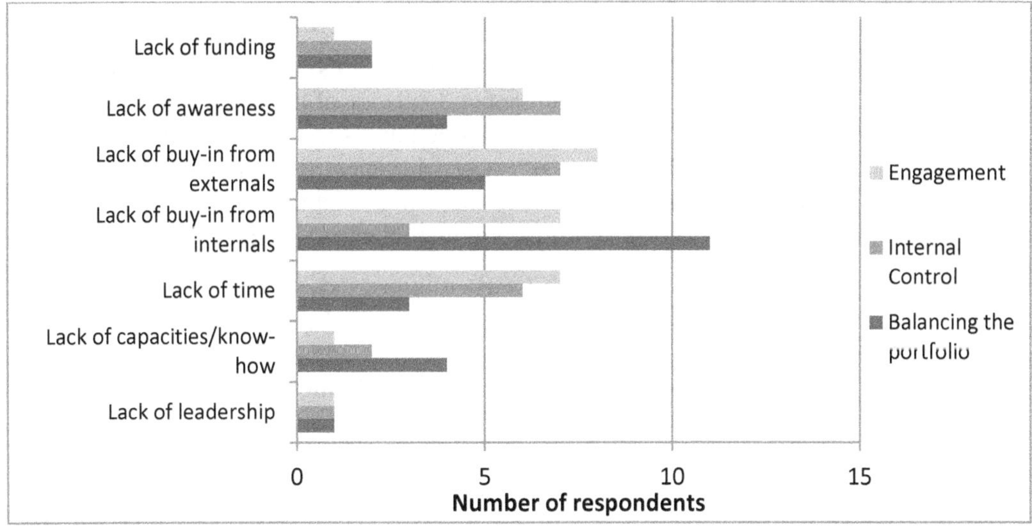


These findings suggest that the CGR may be unified in its approaches and aims for internal control, but that there is resistance or obstacles to be addressed externally, which require time and effort for the CGR. One CGR official pointed to the need to promulgate a better understanding amongst stakeholders of the importance of internal control for improved management of their entities and thus for good governance, accountability and transparency.

An improvement in professional relations and awareness of the respective roles that all public sector actors must play would go a long way to improve the effectiveness of CGR initiatives, reducing tensions between relevant authorities. This requires a commitment and cultural change across government, and is not something that CGR can do on its own.

Despite existing obstacles, there remain other activities that the CGR may undertake in this area. The OECD has gathered suggestions from external stakeholders and combined them with relevant recommendations that remain from the Peer Review. They are as follows:

- Continuing to promote good governance practices, with the caveat that efforts should be made to ensure that suggestions are communicated as potential improvements but not as impositions;
- Providing rankings of audited entities, with a focus on entities that are performing well in terms of following up on observations and complying to provide positive incentives;
- More strategic use of the TdR as positive incentive for "graduating" from TdR, as was recommended in the Peer Review, and as has been exercised through the application of "framework agreements"; and
- Continuing to improve co-operation with the CAIGG for greater clarity in their roles and responsibilities for internal control, and thus of internal audit units whom they are responsible for co-ordinating.

## Alignment and balance of the CGR portfolio

Eighty-four percent of CGR staff surveyed for this progress report found there to be a moderate or substantial change to the alignment and balance of the portfolio. Progress has been made, notably in automating the *ex ante* function and substantiating methodology to broaden its *ex post* function. Yet the CGR faces obstacles in implementing these and other initiatives that would enable the CGR to audit the reliability of financial and non-financial information, and to assess of whole-of-government issues in a systematic way.

Political will was highlighted by both CGR officials and external stakeholders as a barrier to realising change in the alignment and balance of the portfolio. Yet the largest obstacle seen by officials was, in fact, getting buy-in from internal stakeholders, pointing to the need to improve capacity and skills as part of instituting change. To this end, the CGR can build on developments in competency management. Further, collaborations between divisions that will be required by the new performance-evaluation system for CGR officials should help to ensure cross-cutting observations are backed by CGR officials in a more unified way.

It appears that there has been a change in the approach of the CGR towards public administration, demonstrating a greater willingness to shift responsibility of *ex ante* control of legality to control units. Stakeholders suggest that the communication around any such adjustments should employ a collaborative and educational tone to continue to reduce the perception of the CGR as punitive and compliance oriented.

The CGR has made efforts to generate a greater understanding, on the part of its stakeholders, in the CGR's work. Heightened frequency of interaction has the reciprocal benefit of enabling the CGR to gather in-depth information on stakeholder needs that can be better integrated into CGR work and priorities. Increased awareness on the part of both parties is needed to retain relevance of audit work, to elevate the findings to the attention of decision-makers and to ensure that findings are well understood once brought to their attention.

Auditees reported that the consolidated products that promote best practices and lessons from across the public sector have been useful. The CGR could further expand and disseminate these new value-added products to foster a greater awareness of the importance of effectiveness, efficiency and economy for the public administration in this 21st century, thereby familiarising CGR officials and stakeholders further with elements that would underline future performance assessments.

# Notes

1 As of February 18, progress on audits can be found on the Citizen Portal (*Contraloría y Ciudadano*) under the Audit Plan for 2015 "PLAN OPERATIVO DE AUDITORIAS 2015", http://www.contraloria.cl/NewPortal2/portal2/ShowProperty/BEA%20Repository/Sitios/Ciudadano/Contribuya.

2 At the time of the OECD review only 25% of Chilean households had access to broadband internet, while the OECD average was 67%, as discussed in "Chile's Supreme Audit Institution", page 238.

3 At the time of the Review, the SAIs of Australia, Denmark, the European Union, Italy, Portugal, South Africa and Spain have auditee strategies, as discussed in "Chile's Supreme Audit Institution", Table 4.3, page 218.

4 As documented in the OECD Peer Review, the *ex ante* audit function did not exist in the majority of benchmark SAIs, while in the few where it was present, the scope is limited, either functionally (e.g. Italy) or financially (e.g. Portugal).

5 Some CGR officials saw a moderate or substantial change (22% respectively).

6 Law 20 766, of July 2014.

7 An exception are the financial audits of supply companies in isolated areas (EMAZA) and of the loans facilitated to Chile by multilateral financial institutions, such as the Inter-American Development Bank or the World Bank.

# *Bibliography*

CGR (2015), *Strategic Report: Implementation Status of Key Recommendations made by the OECD to the Office of the Comptroller General of the Republic of Chile*, CGR, Santiago.

CGR (2014a), *Estimación del Valor Económico del Control Fiscal Superior: El Caso de la Contraloría General de la República de Chile*, CGR, Santiago.

CGR (2014b), *Newsletter No. 5: December*, IPSAS Accounting Analysis Division, CGR, Santiago.

GfK Adimark (2013), *Informe Barómetro de Acceso a Información, 2013* [Access to Information Barometer Report, 2013] GfK Adimark, Chile, accessible at www.anp.cl/images/docs/Resultados%20Bar%C3%B3metro%202013_VF.pdf.

INTOSAI (2010), *How to Increase the Use and Impact of Audit Reports: A Guide for Supreme Audit Institutions*, INTOSAI Capacity Building Committee, http://cbc.courdescomptes.ma.

Libertad y Desarrollo (2014), *Encuesta de Corrupción 2014* [Corruption Survey, 2014], Libertad y Desarrollo, Chile, accesible at: http://lyd.org/wp-content/themes/LYD/files_mf/encuestadecorrupci%C3%83%C2%93n2014.pdf.

OECD (2014), *Chile's Supreme Audit Institution: Enhancing strategic agility and public trust*, OECD Public Governance Reviews, OECD Publishing, Paris, http://dx.doi.org/10.1787/9789264207561-en

# ORGANISATION FOR ECONOMIC CO-OPERATION AND DEVELOPMENT

The OECD is a unique forum where governments work together to address the economic, social and environmental challenges of globalisation. The OECD is also at the forefront of efforts to understand and to help governments respond to new developments and concerns, such as corporate governance, the information economy and the challenges of an ageing population. The Organisation provides a setting where governments can compare policy experiences, seek answers to common problems, identify good practice and work to co-ordinate domestic and international policies.

The OECD member countries are: Australia, Austria, Belgium, Canada, Chile, the Czech Republic, Denmark, Estonia, Finland, France, Germany, Greece, Hungary, Iceland, Ireland, Israel, Italy, Japan, Korea, Luxembourg, Mexico, the Netherlands, New Zealand, Norway, Poland, Portugal, the Slovak Republic, Slovenia, Spain, Sweden, Switzerland, Turkey, the United Kingdom and the United States. The European Union takes part in the work of the OECD.

OECD Publishing disseminates widely the results of the Organisation's statistics gathering and research on economic, social and environmental issues, as well as the conventions, guidelines and standards agreed by its members.

OECD PUBLISHING, 2, rue André-Pascal, 75775 PARIS CEDEX 16
(42 2016 01 1 P) ISBN 978-92-64-25189-2 – 2016

www.ingramcontent.com/pod-product-compliance
Lightning Source LLC
LaVergne TN
LVHW081424110826
845149LV00010B/1865
* 9 7 8 9 2 6 4 2 5 1 8 9 2 *